CHRISTMAS
PROGRAM BUILDER
No. 50

A Graded Collection of Resources for the
Creative Program Planner

Compiled by Paul M. Miller

Permission to make noncommercial photocopies
of Program Builder material is granted to the
purchaser when three books have been pur-
chased. The photocopies cannot be sold, loaned,
or given away.

D1715167

KANSAS CITY, MO 64141

Preschool

Welcome

Ladies and gentlemen,
Family and friends;
Glad you are with us,
'Til our program ends.
—*P.M.M.*

It's Christmastime

It is Christmas!
Let us rejoice;
Praising Jesus,
With heart and voice.
—*Cora M. Owen*

Holy Birth

CHILD 1: Jesus came to earth.
What a holy birth!

CHILD 2: He was God's own Son.
What a holy One!
—*Cora M. Owen*

I Can't Say Much

I'm a little shy, so I can't say much.
On Christmas Day, may you feel
His touch.
—*Nancy Merical*

I Love Jesus

I'm here tonight [today] to stand and
say,
I love Jesus, born on Christmas Day.
—*Nancy Merical*

Stop, Look, and Listen

CHILD 1: Stop, everybody. Stop and
spend awhile.
Enjoy our Christmas program, we'll
do it up in style.

CHILD 2: Look, everybody. Look at
who we are.
We're your Christmas program,
we're kids from near and far.

CHILD 3: Listen, everybody. Listen
to what we say.
Hear the story of Jesus, who was
born on Christmas Day.
—*P.M.M.*

A Christmas Recipe

*(Child enters in apron and carrying
a large mixing bowl. He or she stirs
with a big wooden spoon.)*
I'm not making sugar cookies,
Or the best brownies found on
earth.
I'm stirring up a program,
About Jesus and His birth.
—*P.M.M.*

A Gift

*(Child enters carrying a very large
wrapped Christmas present.)*
I like Christmas presents.
Big ones and even small.
But don't forget our Jesus,
The best Present of them all.
—*P.M.M.*

The Animals of Christmas

(Children wear touches of costume to represent the animals mentioned. Make this as elaborate or simple as resources allow.)

CHILD 1 (donkey): If I were the donkey,
   that carried his mother,
I'd stay close beside Him,
   like He was my brother.

CHILD 2 (cow): If I were the cow,
   that stood by His bed,
I'd give Jesus some milk,
   without any bread.

CHILD 3 (lamb): If I were a lamb,
   all fuzzy and white,
I'd give Jesus my wool,
   so warm and so bright.

CHILD 4 (dove): If I were a dove,
   in the rafters above,
I'd coo Jesus a song,
   about His Father's love.

CHILD 5 (camel): If I were a camel,
   with humps and so tall,
I'd go to my knees,
   and guard Jesus so small.

CHILD 6 (kitten): If I were a kitty,
   all furry and warm,
Jesus would cuddle beside me;
   I'd keep Him from harm.

CHILD 7 (dog): If I were a dog,
   with a great loud bark,
I'd stand by the manger,
   when it got dark.

BOYS: We're none of us animals,

GIRLS: We're just girls and boys;

ALL: We'll tell Jesus we love Him,
   With our animal noise.

(Each child makes own animal sound.)

—*P.M.M.*

What Christmas Is All About

(For three little children)

CHILD 1: Away in a manger a baby lay,
Long, long ago on Christmas Day.

CHILD 2: While shepherds watched their sheep at night,
They saw an angel shining bright.

CHILD 3: The shepherds went to see the child
With His mother, all meek and mild.

—*P.M.M.*

Welcome

I can't talk loud;
   I'm kinda small,
But I've been asked
   To welcome all.

—*P.M.M.*

Little Jesus

Jesus was a baby sweet,
   Born so long ago,
Jesus is our Savior, who
   Wants us to love Him so.

—*Felix White*

Joy

(For three children who hold letters J, O, and Y)

CHILD 1 ("J"): Jesus is born,

CHILD 2 ("O"): On a bed of hay.

CHILD 3 ("Y"): You need to love Him.

ALL: Happy Christmas Day!

—*Velda Blumhagan*

I'm a Little Innkeeper

Lord Jesus, I'm a little innkeeper
Who has found room for You
To live in my heart
All the year through.

—Nancy Merical

Christmas Bells

(Children ring small bells as they enter. One child steps forward and recites.)
Can you hear our bells.
Ringing loud and clear?
Reminding us all,
That Christmastime is here?

—Cynthia Boles

I'm So Small

I'm too small for great big words,
But what I'm here to say,
Will be the biggest words you've
ever heard;
(Shout)
Jesus was born on Christmas Day!

—Nancy Merical

A Question

Do you know why Jesus came?
He was sent from heaven above,
As a gift from God, with love.
(Throws a big kiss to audience)

—Nancy Merical

H-O-P-E

(An acrostic for four children who carry large letters)

CHILD 1 ("H"): Hosanna in the highest

CHILD 2 ("O"): On earth, peace among men.

CHILD 3 ("P"): Promise of peace is given

CHILD 4 ("E"): Each Christmas, again and again.

—Velda Blumhagen

Ages 6 to 8

Christmas Means a Lot

Christmas means a lot to me;
Presents waiting beneath a tree.
Still, the best gift comes from God
 above—
Jesus sent to show the Father's
 love.

—Nancy Merical

A Choral Speech for First Graders

(Children decorate tree as they speak.)

CHILD 1: Here are some ornaments
 red and blue.

CHILD 2: Here is some tinsel of sil-
 very hue.

CHILD 3: Here are some lights to
 string on our tree.
See how they shine as bright as can
 be.

CHILD 4: Now, here are more ornaments, green and gold,
And fine decorations, so nice to be-
 hold.

CHILD 5 *(tallest):* And then at last,
 for the highest place,
Here is an angel with a lovely face.
And next to the angel, a star to
 shine
And glow in the dark as a special
 sign.

ALL: This tree reminds us that
 God's love is near.
That the Babe in the manger is fi-
 nally here.

—Jean Conder Soule

Christmas All Year Long

Go and find someone each day,
 A person you can cheer.
And give to them some Christmas joy,
 That will last them through the
 year.

—P.M.M.

The Light of Christmas

Put a candle in the window
 And string lights of every hue,
To remind us of the Light
 Who came at Christmas for me and
 you.

—P.M.M.

Come with Love

In a manger filled with hay,
Christ our little King did lay.
Come with joy,
Let us pray.

—Robert Colbert

Brand New

A brand-new baby boy is born,
To give us joy on Christmas morn.
So let's all do our very best,
To make this day His happiest.

—Robert Colbert

Just a Little Kid

I'm just a little kid,
    I haven't much to say;
But I'm so very happy,
    Because it's Christmas Day.
        —*Robert Colbert*

Jesus, Our Savior

CHILD 1: A star shone so brightly
one night
That wise men traveled by its light.

CHILD 2: They searched for a baby
in Bethlehem,
Promised to become the Savior of
men.

CHILD 3: When they found Him,
they knelt with joy,
Giving gifts to this baby boy.

CHILD 4: Then they returned the
way they came,
Knowing they would never forget
His name.

CHILD 5: His name was Jesus, the
Savior of us all,
Sent to earth to redeem and to call.
        —*Nancy Merical*

The Lasting Gift

*(Student carries a Bible and opens it
on third line)*

A Christmas gift that lasts forever,
    Lots of people don't receive;
This gift can be found in the Word
    of God—
    It's salvation for all who will be-
    lieve.
        —*Iris Gray Dowling*

Happy Birthday, Jesus

CHILD 1: I would like to have been a
shepherd boy
On that long-ago night,
Visited by angels in robes of pure
white.

CHILD 2: I would like to have been a
wise man,
Led by a gleaming star,
Leading them to Bethlehem from
the East so far.

CHILD 3: I would like to have been
Joseph
There by a rustic manger,
Protecting Baby Jesus, from harm
and any danger.

CHILD 4: I would like to have been
Mary,
Holding Jesus in my arms,
A mother oh so sweet and good,
keeping Him from harm.

ALL: We couldn't be there that holy
night,
But still we can follow in His light.
And we can make Christmas more
bright,
By wishing Him a happy birthday
tonight.
*(All children sing "Happy birthday,
dear Jesus.")*
        —*Nancy Merical*

A Message

We want to close our program
    With a message from all of us.
May every person here
    Have a very Merry Christmas.
        —*Beverly Ann Hoffeditz*

Ages 9 to 11

My Gift

My gift is not like most.
    It is not here to see.
I have not special-wrapped it,
    To put beneath the tree.
The gift I have for Mary's baby,
    Is the best that I have—it's me!
                                —*P.M.M.*

A Christmas Dialogue

BOY *(carrying a toy):* Boy, oh boy, oh boy! Look at this [name toy]. I've been saving my allowance for three months and have recycled stuff all fall, just so I could buy it.

GIRL *(entering):* [Boy's name], is that your gift for the Jesse tree?

BOY: The what-kind-of-a-tree?

GIRL: The Jesse tree! What's wrong with you, don't you listen in church?

BOY: Well, actually . . .

GIRL *(interrupting):* A Jesse tree is a special Christmas tree for gifts that you are giving to people with special needs.

BOY: Oh, yeah, now I remember—I think.

GIRL: Oh, the boy in that missionary family will just love that [toy].

BOY: Yeah, but . . .

GIRL *(interrupting again):* In fact, I think it was on his wish list.

BOY: Well sure, but . . .

GIRL *(interrupting):* Oh, [name], that's so kind of you to be so generous. Wait till I tell the other girls. (GIRL *exits.*)

BOY *(quiet for a moment):* Well, why not? A missionary's kid, huh? I guess it is pretty generous of me. Sure, why not? I'll do it. But, what in the world is a Jesse tree? *(Exits)*
                                —*P.M.M.*

I Remember

God, when I see a shining star
Way up in the sky so far,
I remember the Star of Bethlehem
That shone so bright
On that first holy Christmas night,
Leading wise men to you.

So when I look up in the sky
And see the stars you've placed so
    high,
Help me remember why Jesus
    came.
And keep Christmas, from the start,
What it should be within my heart,
Leading children to You.
                        —*Nancy Merical*

What Christmas Means to Me

CHILD 1: What is Christmas?

CHILD 2: We'll try to explain;

CHILD 3: Christmas is more
Than bicycles and trains.

CHILD 4: More than stockings and
gifts
Waiting beneath the tree.

CHILD 5: More than all the lights
And decorations you see.

CHILD 1: Christmas is love and
peace and joy;
All wrapped up in a Baby Boy.

CHILD 2: Christmas is the birthday
of Jesus our King;
Wow! That's a thought to make us
sing!

*(Group sings chorus of "Oh, How I
Love Jesus.")*

—*Nancy Merical*

Why He Came

When I look all around me,
I see all the lights aglow;
I think of Jesus in Bethlehem,
Born in a manger long ago.

I know God's only begotten Son
Came to this world below;
To bring salvation for me
Because He love me so.

—*Iris Gray Dowling*

The Manger Scene

*(Children may assemble a crèche as
they recite the following.)*

CHILD 1: Here is the manger rudely
built.

CHILD 2: But where is the baby's
pretty quilt?

CHILD 3: Oh! He has no comforter
for His bed
And no pillow soft to cradle His
head.

CHILD 4: But look, there's plenty of
clean yellow straw.
My, this is the strangest crib I ever
saw.

CHILD 5: See those shepherds, with
their little white sheep;
Watching the babe as He lies
asleep.

CHILD 6: And hear the angels
singing a song,
A lullaby hymn for all night long.

CHILD 7: Mary, His mother, is lying
there.
Isn't it nice that she will share
Her precious Son with all the earth?
Our Savior and the Prince of Peace.

CHILD 8: So, here is stable, and up
above,
As a promise of our Father's love;
See the shining star poised very
still,
In the Christmas sky above the hill.

—*Jean Conder Soule*

Christ Has Come

(Children hold cutout letters)
C Cradled in a manger stall,
H Heralded by the angel's call,
R Redeemer of Jews and Gentiles alike,
I Is the Baby Jesus this Christmas night.
S Shepherds adore the infant mild,
T Then tell their world of the Holy Child.

H Heaven to earthly man has bent,
A And new hope and joy is sent.
S So, let us come on bended knee.

C Come to the manger and see the King.
O Oh, worship the One who'll make the world sing . . .
M Messiah, Redeemer, our Savior is He,
E Emmanuel, God with us; oh, come now and see!

ALL: Christ has come!
—Mary W. Fensternmacher

The Star

There was a star that shone so
 bright
In the sky that cloudless night;
God gave the wise men living sight
As they gazed upon His heavenly
 light.
—Iris Gray Dowling

Tell of Jesus' Birth

Come sing the Christmas songs
 That tell of Jesus' birth;
So many have not heard
 Why Jesus came to earth.
—Iris Gray Dowling

Christmas Prayer

O Christmas star, you shine so
 bright
And tell us of that holy night,
When Christ was born so long ago,
Amid the stable and manger low.

O Christmas star, your heavenly
 glow
Tells of God's love and mercy He'd
 show.
Love that reaches down to man's
 pain and strife;
Love that endures throughout the
 lonely night.

Thank You, dear Father, for Your
 heavenly Gift,
As upward to Thee, our faces we
 lift.
Help us be worthy of the love You
 bestow,
As we travel life's journey on earth
 here below.
—Mary W. Fenstermacher

Jesus Waits for You

You don't need to travel to Bethle-
 hem
 Jesus Christ is not there.
He's in heaven patiently waiting
 To hear your humble prayer.
—Iris Gray Dowling

9

Don't Leave Him Out

(For a child with a long Christmas list with the name "Jesus," written in large letters at the top. This is shown at the end.)

We celebrate a special day,
  The birthday of a King.
We shop and spend for many gifts,
  But don't give Him a thing.

We always seem to leave Him out,
  When the presents we exchange;
And never have Him as our guest,
  When parties we arrange.

So let's decide to make the Lord,
  The first name on our list;
And bring a gift of love to Him.
  Don't let His name be missed.

          —Cora M. Owen

God's Gifts

Cookies cooling on a rack;
A toy train whistling 'round the
  track
  Beneath the Christmas tree.

Children caroling in the mall;
Snowflakes gliding as they fall
  On the lawn and on the lea.

Bells that chime on a cold clear
  night;
Stars that stud the sky with light,
  And a moon glitter the sea.

Each is a gift from the Lord above,
Who came as a Babe to share His
  love
  With you and you and me.
(Points to people on last line)

          —Margaret Primrose

True Joy

Jesus is God's eternal gift,
  Sent to us long ago;
You need to receive Him as Savior,
  If true joy you want to know.

          —Iris Gray Dowling

Unwanted

A Monologue for Christmas Meditation
John 1:11

by Robert Allen

I looked today into the face of an unborn child and knew what it was to be unwanted. It was a sad face, sadder than any child's face deserves to be. His eyes seemed ancient, reflecting as they did the pain of rejection that he had experienced but did not understand. His arms reached out for someone to love—someone, anyone to care.

No one wanted him. The man who planned to marry his mother didn't want him. Repelled by the prospect of raising a child he had not fathered, he had decided to call off the marriage. The child wasn't his responsibility. Besides, he had his future to consider. Children were a great expense, and in this case, an unwanted expense.

His mother didn't want him. She faced shame and humiliation at finding herself pregnant and still unmarried. This child didn't fit into her plans. It just wasn't the right time. She was poor and couldn't afford to raise a child on her own. He was a burden to her, already a grief to her heart, though still unborn.

Society didn't want him either, and they had a solution. Get rid of him. If government approval was attained, that made it legal. And the government did approve. After all, they reasoned, it was better for everyone concerned that an unwanted child not be brought into the world. He would simply further complicate an already stressed-out society. He would be in the way. He would be a burden to the tax-paying public. Better to eliminate the problem early than allow him to grow up and die a criminal's death.

I looked today into the face of an unborn child, the unborn Christ child. It was a face of sorrow, acquainted with grief. It sorrowed for every unborn and unwanted child who is rejected by an uncaring society. It mourned for every man and woman to whom approaching parenthood seemed a burden too difficult to face. It lamented for every nation that would choose to destroy rather than protect its future.

As I looked into those eyes of the Christ child, just longing to be loved, I thought: Are we so different today? Though unwanted by His own people, He came to them anyway, because He was just what they needed. Today, He is still the One the whole world needs. And today He is still unwanted.

Today, I looked into the face of an unborn child, and together we wept.

The Innkeeper's Wife Speaks

A Monologue

by Grace Reese Adkins

I should not have sent her away,
　So tired, so worn;
I think her expected Babe
　Was about to be born.
Who knows how far she had come,
　From what distant land
To enroll for the tax of Judah's tribe
　At Caesar's command?

Where did she spend the night?
　On a spot of ground
with only the stars for light
　And the cattle 'round,
Breathing their warm, sweet breath
　In the stable's gloom,
And a sense as of life and death
　In the lowly room.

But the silence broke with a song
　Never heard before,
And it floated the stars among
　To the stable door.
"Hosanna," it seemed to say,
　"In the highest heaven
For God to the earth today
　A Savior has given."

The Gift

A Monologue-Like Piece for Christmas

by Daniel Wray

Production notes: This theatre piece is designed to be performed by a multigenerational cast, although it can be staged by youth groups.

Costumes: All characters are in contemporary dress, with kids in foot pajamas. John Henry and the Narrator should both have heavy coats.

Props: A coatrack, large old rocking chair, a Christmas tree and decorations, some wrapped presents, and the "gift" (should be a fairly homely package showing sign of years of wear).

Setting: Set requirements are minimal. No special lighting is necessary; the play may easily be performed in the sanctuary-chancel area.

Cast of Characters:

NARRATOR: *Male or female. Has obvious affection for the people he or she refers to and is warmly nostalgic.*

JOHN HENRY: *A lovable elderly gentleman, although the role may be adapted to be an elderly female. He is involved and dramatic in his storytelling.*

CHILD 1 and CHILD 2: *Typical 6- to 10-year-olds who are thoroughly engrossed in John Henry's story. Respectful.*

OTHER CHILDREN: *Audience of typical children who are engrossed in the story. These are nonspeaking parts, though you may divide the speaking parts for Child 1 and Child 2 and assign to other kids.*

At rise, a Christmas tree stands stage left. Under the tree are wrapped presents. The NARRATOR *comes up the center aisle, wearing a wireless mike that enables freedom to wander. He or she holds a small, tattered and yellowed package. It is wrapped in plain paper or newsprint—it should look at least 75 years old.* NARRATOR *carries the package to center stage and sets it down careful to remove his or her coat. Once coat is off, he or she places it over the back of a chair, stage right, then carefully retrieves the package, looks at it, and smiles. He or she notices the audience and acknowledges them.*

NARRATOR: Good evening, and merry Christmas. *(Pause)* Ah, Christmas! There aren't too many folks around who don't love Christmas. After all, there's the warm glow that you get when you reminisce about the glorious Christmases of the past. I'm no exception, as you'll soon find out. *(Walks over to chair and is seated)* Oh, I suppose you're wondering about this here gift. *(Laughs quietly to self)* It sure doesn't look like much, does it? Ah, but you'd be surprised. *(Holds it up and inspects it)* The wrapping has yellowed, to be sure, but it's still remarkably intact for a package of its age. As John Henry would say, it came from a time when *(affects voice to mimic older man)* "you got paid cash for a hard day's work." *(Smiles, pausing to remember)* None of us could really imagine such a day, but John Henry had a convincing way about him, so we always remained respectfully silent. The package is still put under our tree year after year, although the man who first placed it there is long gone. And year after year we tell the story that he used to tell, and we remember the gift that he gave us all.

(NARRATOR rises with the package and walks over to the tree to place it underneath as he or she speaks.)

Two things were certain on Christmas Eve when I was younger; one was the aroma of freshly baked Christmas cookies that filled the house by early afternoon. The other was that right before supper, John Henry would come through the door with his arms full of presents. He was grandfather to the whole neighborhood—a strange, happy man who lived down the road. It was rumored that he hadn't actually cooked a meal in years; he preferred to coordinate his visits to coincide with mealtimes at various homes in the area. But nobody seemed to mind. He had a mystical quality about him that drew genuine benevolence from people, and they were grateful to him for bringing that part of them to the surface.

(During a brief pause, the other characters take their places on stage. JOHN HENRY on the far right, with CHILDREN gathered around him listening in rapt attention. JOHN HENRY mimes telling a story to the children.)

John Henry usually spoke rapidly, but when it came time for storytelling, his voice became deliberate and low; it created a reverence in the room that was magnified by the attentive silence. John Henry always told two stories on Christmas Eve, but he would preface them with, "If you listen very carefully, you'll only hear one." The first story was about a baby who was born in a stable somewhere, and the commotion he caused.

(JOHN HENRY *stands and goes to the tree. He picks up the gift while* CHILDREN *watch. He brings it back to his chair and is seated.*)

For his second story, John Henry would always move over to the tree and pick up this same present that's been under our tree. He held the gift so reverently that young and old alike were breathless with anticipation. We sat and stared at the small wrapped box and then at John Henry. Finally, he would begin the story—oh so softly and low.

JOHN HENRY: When I was no higher than . . . this little one here . . .

NARRATOR: He always picked the smallest child in the room.

JOHN HENRY: I couldn't wait for Christmas! Why, I remember sometimes going to bed before it was even dark, just so morning would come faster, and I could open my present.

CHILD 1: Really?

JOHN HENRY: Oh, I did! I couldn't wait.

NARRATOR: The firelight danced in his smiling eyes.

JOHN HENRY: Mama and Daddy always dressed the tree with lighted candles and strings of popcorn and berries—it was almost as pretty as your tree. Anyhow, one Christmas I was really hoping for something. I was so excited. I remember asking over and over again, "Mama, I've been good this year , ain't I?" And she always answered, "Yes, John Henry, you've been a real good boy." And then she'd smile kinda sadlike and tell me to go out to play.

CHILD 2: What was it that you were hoping for? A bike?

CHILD 1: No, I bet it was a Power Ranger.

JOHN HENRY: Oh, heavens, no!

NARRATOR: Said John Henry, wondering what on earth a Power Ranger was.

JOHN HENRY: See, times were hard, and we were really poor. Why, I felt lucky just to get a present at all. That's right, just one! Now, let's see, what was it I got that year? Yes, I remember what it was. It was a slingshot. *(Pleased with himself)* Imagine that! Remembering after all this time.

NARRATOR: Every year John Henry "remembered after all this time."

JOHN HENRY: That Christmas was especially hard 'cause the summer had been hot and the crops had shriveled up like the skin on an old peach. Mama and Daddy told me that maybe they couldn't get me anything for Christmas, but I never really believed them 'cause there were always presents under the tree before. And sure enough, this present *(holds it up)* appeared under our tree with my name on it.

NARRATOR: He stopped to let everyone gaze on the package before continuing.

JOHN HENRY: All week long I picked up my package—just to feel it, shake it a little, to try to figure out if it was my slingshot or not. It felt so good just to have a package of my very own.

CHILD 2: Was it a slingshot?

JOHN HENRY: I'm getting there, just hold your horses. Anyway, by the time Christmas Eve finally rolled around, I was so excited I couldn't sleep. I could hardly wait to open that package—to see if it really was my slingshot.

CHILD 1: Over a dumb old slingshot?

JOHN HENRY: Not *just* a slingshot! It was *my* slingshot. Haven't you ever hoped for something so much that you thought you might explode? Well, I decided I couldn't wait. I got up in the middle of the night—Christmas Eve, mind you, and started to sneak downstairs to see if I could open the box through the bottom, real careful-like, so my folks wouldn't know . . .

CHILD 2: Did you?

JOHN HENRY: Well, I sneaked halfway down the stairs—real quiet-like, that's when I saw Mama and Daddy. The room was all a yellow glow from the candles on the tree, and shadows were dancing across the wall and the fireplace. Mama and Daddy were talking real sad and soft, like when Gretchen our milk cow died. I tried not to listen, but I heard my name. Mama said, "We should have told him sooner—he'll be so disappointed." At first I couldn't understand what they were talking about 'cause I had a present, just like always. But after awhile, I figured out that there wasn't anything in the box. It was just full of rags or something.

CHILD 1: They tricked you?

JOHN HENRY: That's exactly what I thought. So, I sneaked back upstairs, got into bed, and just cried my pillow wet. But then I started thinking . . .

CHILD 2: About what?

JOHN HENRY: About why my parents would fool me like that. I thought about how excited I had been about opening my present. And then when I thought about it again, I got all excited all over again, and felt warm inside. After awhile I realized that it wasn't really the slingshot that had made me excited at all, it was that I had something to look forward to! And I thought, "Mama and Daddy must really love me to give me something to hope for."

CHILD 1: But what happened Christmas morning?

JOHN HENRY: Well, I got up remembering everything I had thought about the night before, and I ran downstairs. Mama and Daddy heard me and rushed into the front room where the tree was. They wanted to keep me from opening my present and being really disappointed. I just sat down next to my present and smiled. Mama said, "John Henry, I'm afraid . . . I'm afraid we couldn't get you anything this year. That box is empty." And do you know what I told her?

CHILD 1 and 2: What?

JOHN HENRY: I said, "No it isn't, Mama. This box is full of hope!" Then my mama and my daddy started to cry, but older folks sometimes do that when there's not really anything to be sad about, so it was OK.

CHILD 2: You really never opened the present?

JOHN HENRY: That's right. I kept my present and never opened it 'cause it made me feel good whenever I saw it. I knew it had a lot of love in it.

(All characters freeze for blackout or exit.)

NARRATOR *(rises and strolls over to pick up the package; then returns to center stage):* That was always where the story ended, although some of the younger ones wanted to argue with him. He just nibbled on cookies and smiled, winking at the older folks. I kept the gift, because I wanted to remember the story—because I know there's still a present in there. The best kind at Christmas—*hope!*

(Blackout)

The Christmas Mistake

by Iris Gray Dowling

Theme: Unappreciated kindness. Two boys work hard to earn money for a gift for their invalid sister, only to discover she doesn't want it.

Cast of Characters:

TREVOR: *Debbie's brother*

JEREMY: *Debbie's other brother*

DEBBIE: *the boys' invalid sister*

MOM

DAD

Setting: All scenes take place in the dining room.

Props: Wrapped presents, money, Christmas tree, dishes, table, chairs, bags of presents or food, wheelchair

Scene 1

(The dining room two weeks before Christmas. At rise, TREVOR *and* JEREMY *are sitting at the table writing out their Christmas lists.)*

JEREMY: Debbie said she wanted a Bible computer game. I feel sorry for her stuck in that wheelchair most of the time.

TREVOR: Yeah, if she had one, she could play with it when we're busy.

JEREMY: I think that's a great present to get her.

TREVOR: But how? It costs more money than we have.

JEREMY: Maybe we can get a job raking leaves . . .

TREVOR: Or cleaning the neighbors' garages.

JEREMY: Yeah, or how about if it snows, we can shovel walks and driveways.

TREVOR: Maybe we ought to talk this over with Mom and Dad.

JEREMY: Why, bro?

TREVOR: They need to know where we are when we're working.

JEREMY: Yeah, I guess you're right.

TREVOR: OK, we'll talk to them as soon as they get home.

JEREMY *(looking out the window):* Hey, here they are right now.

MOM and DAD *(entering the room):* Hi, kids.

(They set their grocery bags on the table. DAD exits and returns with more bags.)

JEREMY and TREVOR: Hi, Mom . . . Dad.

TREVOR: We really need to talk to you.

DAD *(setting bags on table):* What's the matter? Is something wrong, boys?

JEREMY: No, we just want to surprise Debbie with a Christmas gift—

TREVOR *(interrupting):* A Bible computer game!

JEREMY: We'll earn money by working for the neighbors.

DAD: Do you think you can earn enough? That's a pretty expensive undertaking.

MOM: Do you know how much those games cost?

TREVOR: We can work hard.

JEREMY: We wanted you to know why we wouldn't be home sometimes.

MOM: I'm glad you told us. I like your idea.

JEREMY: Please don't tell Debbie. We want to surprise her.

DAD: All right, boys. We'll keep your secret.

(MOM *and* DAD *exit into the kitchen.)*

JEREMY: Well, so far so good. Now we have to find some jobs.

(Blackout)

Scene 2

(Same scene, two days later. MOM *and* DAD *are setting the table.* JEREMY *counts his money at the table.)*

DAD: Is Trevor home yet?

MOM: I haven't seen him.

JEREMY: We worked on two different neighbors' jobs.

TREVOR *(entering):* Hi, Dad, Mom, I sure am hungry.

JEREMY: It's about time you got here.

TREVOR: Boy, the food smells so good, and I'm so tired.

DAD: How much money did you boys earn today?

TREVOR: I got a couple of dollars for that last job.

JEREMY *(waving money):* I've made $10 so far.

TREVOR: And I've got $10.

*(*DEBBIE *wheels in from the right.)*

DEBBIE: What are you guys talking about?

TREVOR and JEREMY *(stuffing money into their pockets):* Nothing!

DEBBIE: It sounded like something to me. *(Rather cross)* I don't know why everyone shuts up when I come around.

JEREMY: It's just your imagination, Sis.

MOM *(coming in from kitchen):* Debbie, it's time for dinner.

DEBBIE *(ignoring* MOTHER*):* And besides that, why haven't you been playing with me lately?

TREVOR: We don't have time . . .

JEREMY *(interrupting):* Ah—we've been busy.

DEBBIE: Busy? Doing what?

JEREMY *(before* TREVOR *can answer):* We're helping one of the neighbors . . .

TREVOR *(finishing for his brother):* Put up his Christmas lights on the house.

DEBBIE *(peevishly):* They must have lots of lights. I haven't seen very much of you.

JEREMY *(changing the subject):* Well, here we are now—take a look.

DEBBIE *(ignoring him):* So why were you working so hard for a neighbor?

TREVOR: We thought maybe he'd give us some money to spend on Christmas presents.

DEBBIE: Well, I want you to spend your time playing with me.

TREVOR: We will as soon as the job's done.

DEBBIE: Well, you're here now. Let's hurry and eat so so you can play a game with me.

TREVOR: OK, Debbie. We'll play right after dinner.

JEREMY *(under his breath to his brother):* Bro, we've gotta finish Mr. Miller's lights.

TREVOR: Oh, brother. Now whata we do?

(Blackout)

Scene 3

(Same scene, one week later. TREVOR and JEREMY are at the table counting their money.)

JEREMY: How much have you earned?

TREVOR: Twenty-five dollars on the nose.

JEREMY: That's great. I've got $30. Now the question is, do we have enough for the game?

TREVOR: We need five more dollars.

JEREMY: Maybe Mom will lend it to us since Christmas is tomorrow.

TREVOR: Maybe we can earn it from her. You know how tired she gets by Christmas Eve.

JEREMY: That's a neat idea, bro.

TREVOR: Let's talk to her now.

(The boys exit.)

(Blackout)

Scene 4

(Christmas morning in the same room. Presents are being opened.)

JEREMY *(under his breath):* OK, Trevor. Get Debbie's package.

(TREVOR *goes to the tree and gets package. The brothers go over to* DEBBIE *in her wheelchair.)*

TREVOR *(handing gift to* DEBBIE): We worked hard to get what you wanted for Christmas.

JEREMY: We sure did.

DEBBIE *(not opening gift, speaks unhappily):* Is that what you've been doing all this time?

JEREMY *(ignoring her unhappiness):* Yep! Trevor and I just want to make you happy.

TREVOR *(anxiously):* Come on, open it, Debbie.

(DEBBIE *opens the present, then frowns.)*

DEBBIE: What's this?

JEREMY *(disappointed):* Whatdaya mean, Debbie?

DEBBIE *(like a spoiled child):* I didn't want this!

TREVOR *(hurt):* You said you did.

DEBBIE *(sulking):* No I didn't! I said I wanted a big doll!

JEREMY: But we worked so hard to get this game . . .

TREVOR: So, you could play it when we aren't around.

DEBBIE: I don't want to stay inside anymore. I want you to take me where you go.

MOM: Come on, dear. You can't go everywhere they go. You know that.

DEBBIE: Yes I can, if they take me! I don't know why I have to stay in this dumb chair, anyway. It's not fair!

(DEBBIE *wheels off angrily.*)

SCENE 5

(Same room later Christmas Day. MOM, DAD, TREVOR, *and* JEREMY *are talking at the table.)*

TREVOR: I can't believe she doesn't like our present.

JEREMY: I'm sure she said she wanted it.

MOM: She did want it.

TREVOR: Maybe if we play with it sometimes, she'll learn to like it.

JEREMY: I say we might as well get some use out of it.

MOM: You know, boys, this makes me think of how some people accept God's special Christmas gift.

TREVOR: How?

MOM: Well, Trevor, who did God send into the world?

TREVOR: That's easy, Jesus.

MOM: Why did He do it, Jeremy?

JEREMY: To save us from our sins?

MOM: Right you are, Son.

TREVOR: Yeah. I know a lot of people who seem like they don't want a Savior.

DAD: The majority of people celebrate Christmas without even thinking about Jesus.

(DEBBIE *starts to enter room in her wheelchair. She stops in doorway and listens. The others don't see her.)*

JEREMY: I get it—they are not willing to accept God's Christmas gift.

MOM: Who was . . .

JEREMY and TREVOR: Jesus!

TREVOR: God must be awfully disappointed when people won't accept Jesus.

JEREMY: Just like I felt when Debbie didn't like our gift.

(DEBBIE *puts her head in her hands.*)

MOM: I know your heart was in the right place, boys . . .

DEBBIE *(wheeling into the room):* Oh, Trevor . . . Jeremy . . . I've been so mean to you.

(The boys look at each other in amazement.)

DEBBIE: I have been so jealous that you two get to go wherever your legs will carry you. And I have to sit in this chair all the time.

(MOM *and* DAD *smile at each other. The brothers go to* DEBBIE.)

DAD: Debbie, if Mom and Trevor and Jeremy and I could give you any gift right now, it would be to enable you to walk again.

DEBBIE *(with head down):* I know, Daddy.

DAD: The church is praying for you, and Dr. Blanchard has the surgery scheduled—

JEREMY *(interrupting):* Trevor and I pray for you every night.

DAD: Good for you, boys. Debbie, since I cannot hand you your healing, I am praying that you will still have peace and joy.

MOM: That's what Christmas is all about, sweetie.

DEBBIE: Will you pray for me right now? Pray that my Christmas gift will be peace and joy.

(The family holds hands in a circle around DEBBIE *and her wheelchair.)*

DAD: Dear Heavenly Father, on this Christmas Eve please give Debbie the best Christmas gift she could ever receive . . .

(Lights slowly fade to blackout.)

By Another Route

An Epiphany Play

by Lauren Glen Dunlap

According to the traditional Church calendar, Epiphany (January 6) is the Sunday, as well as season, that recognizes the manifestation of Christ to the Gentiles. The narrative of the wise men from the East is highlighted.

Cast of Characters:

MELCHOIR

GASPAR

BALTHASAR

After a reading of Matthew 2:1-12, the melody line of "We Three Kings" is heard from the choir loft. Enter from the narthex three wise men dressed in business suits, carrying briefcases. They are the fabled Gaspar (Gas), Balthasar (Bal), and Melchior (Mel). They stop down front on the floor level and variously set or throw down their briefcases.

Opening lines are spoken looking back at where they've come from—a moment of collecting themselves before moving on.

MEL: Well, that's that.

BAL: We found Him.

GAS: The new King of the Jews.

BAL: We paid homage.

GAS: What a King.

(Pause)

GAS: I feel funny.

BAL: So do I

MEL: Maybe we have destination sickness.

BAL: Destination sickness?

MEL *(dramatic and increasing projection):* All those weeks getting ready to travel, then all those weeks following the star and wondering and hoping about the end of our quest and then finally finding Him. The new King of the Jews. *(Drop tone)* I feel funny too.

BAL: It definitely was not what I was expecting.

GAS: Me too. Lack of imagination. Again.

MEL: Well, it's understandable in this instance. You set out to find the new King of the Jews, and instead of ending up in a palace, you wind up in a stable.

BAL: I've never seen an ox or a donkey up close like that.

MEL: And now we go back and let Herod know, right?

GAS: You can't be serious.

BAL: Why not? Of course I'm serious. Why are you looking at me like that?

GAS: We may not agree much on the issues, but I cannot believe you think we ought to go back and tell Herod.

BAL *(with exaggerated patience):* He told us to tell him where to find the new King of the Jews who was to be born. We found Him. Now we tell Herod where to find Him.

MEL *(in a neutral tone, merely observing):* In a stable. With a peasant girl and an unemployed carpenter. Smelling of dust and sweat.

GAS: Do you know what this means?

BAL: What *what* means?

GAS: This baby, this new King of the Jews. This new King born in a wretched stable in a back alley. This new King born to a woman who talks to angels.

MEL: Only one angel. Gabriel is the only one she mentioned.

BAL: You mean the song she sang to put the baby to sleep? "My soul proclaims the greatness of the Lord . . . "? It was just a song. What about it?

GAS: Let me spell it out for you: L-I-B-E-R-A—

MEL: You know I'm not good at spelling in my head, Gaspar.

GAS *(to* MEL*)*: Sorry. *(To* BAL*)* "Liberation."

BAL *(scornfully):* Liberation?

GAS: Think about it. You sure don't have the lowly lifted high unless you also have the powerful dragged off their thrones. You don't have the poor fed unless you also have the rich sent away empty. You think this is something Herod will be *happy* to hear about? You think any of the high-ups at the court or in the Temple will be *tickled* to be told about this? Maybe you think they're just biding their time wielding power until they can resign and devote their lives to acts of mercy? Is that what you think?

MEL: Jimmy Carter did it.

GAS *(to* MEL*)*: We're not talking about Jimmy Carter. *(To* BAL*)* We're talking about Herod. Remember Herod? He's the one who crucified 2,000 people in one fell swoop after that insurrection a while back. He's the one who had his own sons and heirs executed for treason last year.

MEL: I think we should consider the issues here very carefully. You have to look at all sides of the question.

GAS: Sure, but how do you look at all sides when the boundaries just exploded?

BAL: Boundaries are essential, certainly. It's important not to get things mixed up. *(Makes a visible effort to recollect himself)* You've got stables *(gestures left)* and palaces. *(Gestures right. Gestures continue through speech.)* You've got the weak—and the powerful. You've got the human—and the divine. You've got religion—and politics. You've got present—and future. If something is one thing, it can't be something else.

GAS: That may have been true. But not now. And this is just the beginning.

MEL: He was an awfully little baby.

GAS: That's the point. This "awfully little baby" throws everything off balance. It's all upside down, inside out. People won't know their places. They won't know who they are. Are you a Greek or are you a Jew? Are you a slave or are you free? More to the point—are you slave or master? Are you—and this is more frightening than all the rest put together—are you male or are you female? And the answer winds up being—"all of the above." Or, "none of the above."

BAL: Paradox makes for fine rhetoric, but, as you may recall, we were trying to decide the quite practical question of whether or not to report back to Herod.

MEL: No one can say *Herod* doesn't know who he is—that man has an unshakable sense of purpose. Not to mention having a mandate from Caesar. Herod is someone you have to give his due.

GAS: Yes, but what is his due?

BAL: Mel has a point, Gaspar. Herod is a good king.

GAS *(incredulously):* Good? What do you mean by good?

BAL: I mean he's good at what he does. Who else could maintain peace among these justice-obsessed Jews? And I mean he gets things done. He's *effective.* He's built roads through the whole empire; he's erected the new Temple and staffed it; he's maintained law and order. Those were his roads we were traveling on. And you may have noticed that we arrived at our destination with our gifts intact and our skins in one piece.

GAS *(his mind elsewhere than on* BAL'*s words):* How did the words of that lullaby go?

MEL: "You have shown the strength of your arm,
        you have scattered the proud in their conceit.
    You have cast down the mighty from their thrones,
        and have lifted up the lowly.
    You have filled the hungry with good things,
        and the rich you have sent away empty."

GAS: Some lullaby.

MEL: Do you think that's really what she meant, though? There are so many different ways to look at it. Couldn't she have been speaking metaphorically?

BAL *(overly eager):* Yes, I rather thought she was referring to spiritual hunger. Don't you think?

30

GAS *(tired):* Don't ask me. I kept trying to get some clues from Joseph about his take on the baby. But you heard him. He just kept saying, "You'll have to talk to his mother about that."

(Pause)

BAL *(tired):* I don't know.

GAS *(even more tired):* I don't know, either.

MEL: I know! Let's strike a compromise. We won't go back to Herod; we'll just send him a letter.

GAS: Ah, sweet compromise. The worst of both worlds!

BAL: You know, Melchior, sometimes I wish you could just say, "Yes" or "No." Would that be so hard?

MEL: Well, it depends.

(Pause)

MEL: So, do you think they really liked the gifts, or were they just being polite?

BAL: Who can say? The Baby seemed to like your incense better than He liked my gold, anyway. The myrrh seemed a little morbid, if you ask me. I mean, we were visiting a baby, for crying out loud, not preparing someone for burial.

GAS: Birth, death. *(To himself)* Sometimes I think they're not as separate as we think.

MEL: Maybe we should have just gotten a death certificate.

BAL: If you ask me, defying Herod really is not even an option. Whoever that baby is, and will be, is one thing. The fact remains that Herod is the reigning king of the Jews. Defying Herod is simply not a possibility.

GAS: I still think . . .

MEL: Look *(separating them by shoving briefcases into their hands),* lets all just sleep on it. *(All begin to exit.)* Maybe we'll have a fresh perspective on it tomorrow morning.

GAS: OK, but I'm telling you, Herod is not going to be happy if we tell him. *(To himself)* The only thing that would make him more enraged is if we fail to tell him.

BAL: Lighten up, Gaspar. What do you suppose that man's going to do—gather up all the babies in town and slaughter them? Herod may be ruthless, but he couldn't be *that* ruthless.

MEL: Well, good night, you two.

GAS: Good night.

BAL: Sweet dreams.

(From offstage we hear NARRATOR.*)*

NARRATOR: And having been warned in a dream not to go back to Herod, they returned to their country by another route. When they had gone, an angel of the Lord appeared to Joseph in a dream. "Get up," he said, "and take the Child and His mother and escape to Egypt. Stay there until I tell you, for Herod is going to search for the child and kill Him." So Joseph got up, took the child and His mother during the night and left for Egypt. When Herold realized that he had been outwitted by the wise men, he was furious, and he gave orders to kill all the boys in Bethlehem and its vicinity who were two years old and younger, in accordance with the time he had learned from the wise men.

(During continuation of narration, group sings "God Rest Ye Merry, Gentlemen" as underscoring.)

SINGERS *(singing under following narration):* "God rest you merry, gentlemen, let nothing you dismay; remember Christ our Savior was born on Christmas day, to save us all from Satan's power when we were gone astray."

NARRATOR: Then what was said through the prophet Jeremiah was fulfilled: "A voice is heard in Ramah, weeping and great mourning, Rachel weeping for her children and refusing to be comforted, because they are no more."

SINGERS *(in open):* "O tidings of comfort and joy; O tidings of comfort and joy!"

He Really Did Come

by Jerilyn Tyner

Cast of Characters:

BILL: *a 10-year-old boy*

CHRIS: *the baby-sitter, who is 14*

MRS. PAULSON: *a single mother struggling to provide for her kids*

JOEY: *Bill's 5-year-old little brother (or sister)*

DAD: *Chris's father, Mr. Colburn; large man of 40*

Setting is the shabby living room of the Paulson home. Upstage center (UC) is a rather simply decorated Christmas tree; there is a window on the back wall; and outside door stage right (SR). Various childlike Christmas decorations and artwork adorn the room. At rise, BILL and CHRIS are on the couch reading comic books.

BILL: Hey, Chris, I'm tired of lookin' at comic books. Can't we do somethin' else? Can't we go out and make a snow fort or somethin'?

CHRIS: Yeah, that sounds like fun, but your mom made me promise to keep you inside while she takes Joey to the doctor.

BILL: How come?

CHRIS: She doesn't know what's wrong with him, and she's scared you might get sick too—especially if you get wet and cold in the snow.

BILL: Mom's always worried about dumb stuff like that. So, if we have to stay in, what can we do?

CHRIS: For starts, let's turn on the tree lights. Or we could make more paper chains for decorations—or I could help you wrap your mom's present.

BILL: Nah, I already did that in school. *(He picks up paste, paper, and scissors and begins to make paper chain links. CHRIS joins him.)* We made picture frames and decorated them with buttons and ribbon. That's my gift for mom.

CHRIS: Hey, that's neat. What about you? What did you ask Santa to bring you this year?

BILL: Aww, I don't waste my time with that stuff. I don't believe in Santa Claus. I found out a long time ago that it's just your dad, and since my dad ain't here—well, I ain't expectin' much.

CHRIS: But what about Joey?

BILL: Joey? Well, he still believes—at least a little bit. When we put up the tree, he told me that he asked Santa for some Legos and a train set. Then he said that his friend Trevor told him that only babies believe in Santa Claus. Then Joey asked me if I thought Santa would come.

CHRIS: So? What did you tell him?

BILL: I didn't know what to say, you know? And now he's sick, and Mom'll hafta spend money for medicine instead of toys. He's just a little kid, Chris, and it doesn't seem fair. Why'd people go and make up all that dumb junk about Santa comin' down the chimney and making people think there's somethin' so special about Christmas?

CHRIS: Well, Bill, there is something special about Christmas.

BILL: Aw, c'mon. Don't tell me you believe Santa goes around givin' out presents and stuff. Nobody gives anybody somethin' for nothin'.

CHRIS: Bill, I'm not saying Santa brings toys down the chimney, but I know Somebody who gave a Christmas present to everybody in the world. In fact, that's why we have Christmas. And, that's why we give presents—to remind people of the first Christmas present.

BILL: Oh, yeah? What was that?

CHRIS: It wasn't a *what;* it was a *who.*

BILL: Huh? Is this a riddle?

CHRIS: No, just listen. See, God gave the gift of His Son, Jesus. He came as a baby—and He brought gifts for everybody in the world.

BILL: Like what?

CHRIS: Like the gift of peace . . . the gift of kindness to others . . . but most of all, *the* gift—the gift of God's love. People who have God's love quit being selfish. They share God's love. And that's what makes Christmas special—it's when Jesus came into the world.

(The doorbell rings interrupting the boys' conversation. CHRIS opens the door to admit MRS. PAULSON, who carries JOEY in and sets him down on the couch. She takes off her coat.)

MRS. PAULSON: Sorry to have rung the bell, Chris. I couldn't get to my key with Joey in my arms. He still has a fever, and it's so cold . . .

BILL *(peering past her out the door):* Look, it's snowing again. I just gotta find that old sled . . .

CHRIS: How are ya, Joey?

JOEY: I don't feel good, Chris. But I was a good boy at the doctor's. *(He holds out a sticky lollipop.)*

MRS. PAULSON: The doctor says it's his tonsils again. The antibiotics should have him feeling better by tomorrow, but he'll probably need to have those tonsils out.

CHRIS: So, he'll be OK for Christmas?

MRS. PAULSON: Oh, sure, kids bounce back fast. Chris, it's getting pretty late. Do you want me to drive you home?

CHRIS: No problem. My mom called and said Dad'd stop on his way home from work to see if I was ready to leave. *(He glances at his watch.)* He'll probably be along any minute now.

MRS. PAULSON: That'll work out fine, Chris. Give me a few minutes to give Joey his medicine and get him back to bed, and I'll be back with some money for you.

BILL: Hey, Mom, can I *please* go out to the shed and hunt for that sled again?

MRS. PAULSON: Oh, all right. Just be sure you bundle up. Your boots are out in the back porch.

JOEY: When I'm all better, can Chris come over and play with me?

(MOM, JOEY, *and* BILL *exit SL.* BILL *pops back into the room.)*

BILL: Bye, Chris. Will you come over again sometime during vacation to make a snow fort?

CHRIS: Absolutely. (CHRIS *punches* BILL *on the arm to clinch the promise.)*

(BILL *exits SL.* CHRIS *looks thoughtfully around the room as he crosses to couch. Doorbell rings as* CHRIS *starts to sit.* CHRIS *opens the door to admit his* DAD.)

DAD: Well, Son, are you ready to leave yet?

CHRIS: Just about. Bill's mom is putting Joey to bed. She'll be back in a minute to pay me.

(DAD *sits on the edge of the couch holding his hat and brushing off flakes of snow.)*

CHRIS: Y' know, Billy's a pretty decent kid. I don't mind taking care of him and Joey. *(Changing the subject)* Say, Dad, you all ready for Christmas?

DAD *(joking):* Ho, ho, ho! Me and the elves have been working overtime.

CHRIS: I mean, do you have all of your shopping done? Have you got all *my* presents yet?

DAD: Ho, ho, ho! Has Santa ever failed you yet, you greedy little rascal?

CHRIS: C'mon, Dad, be serious. This is important to me.

DAD: OK, Son. I do have one more thing I'm planning to get you. Why?

CHRIS: Well, could you maybe not get me the present and give me the money instead?

DAD: Whaaat? Did you spend all your money? What about the 50 bucks you earned on the tree lot?

CHRIS: Dad, I had a lot of stuff I had to get with that money. I even got you something, if you insist on knowing.

DAD: Hold on, Chris, I never said you had to tell me. I just wonder

36

why you need money so badly that you want to give up some-thing that you've been begging for, for the last six months. *(He stops abruptly, realizing he has given away his surprise.)*

CHRIS *(his face lights up):* It's the computer program I asked for, isn't it, Dad? (DAD *nods.* CHRIS *sighs.)* I've changed my mind about that. It's . . . well, it's not so important to get that right away. I have plenty of fun games, and besides, I have you and Mom—and I have God's love, and . . . well, maybe I'd just like to give a little bit of that away so somebody else will know . . . (CHRIS *obviously feels awkward trying to explain his feelings.)* Well, Dad, I just need to do some more shopping. Can I have the money or not?

DAD *(finally understanding):* Sure, Chris. Let's go home first, and then after supper . . .

(MRS. PAULSON *reenters the room and crosses to* CHRIS. DAD *stands and nods to her.)*

MRS. PAULSON: Hello, Mr. Colburn. This was just about perfect tim-ing, wasn't it? I sure am glad to have someone like your son to sit for my boys. They really like him.

(DAD *acknowledges the praise with a smile.* MRS. PAULSON *turns again to* CHRIS.)

MRS. PAULSON: Thanks for coming, Chris. *(She counts three dollar bills into his hand.)* This isn't much, but I'll try to make it up next time after Christmas.

CHRIS: Hey, don't worry about it. *(He puts on his jacket.)* And you guys have a merry Christmas.

(At the doorway, DAD *and* MRS. PAULSON *exchange good-byes and merry Christmases.* MRS. PAULSON *closes the door.*

(Lights down while soft Christmas music plays during the blackout, indicating a passage of time.

(Lights up. It is early Christmas morning at the Paulson house. Not a creature is stirring, but CHRIS, *stealthily arranging packages under the tree. He has transformed the tree with candy canes and tinsel garlands. Last of all, he arranges a Nativity scene on the table, plugs in the tree lights, then moves quietly to the door. As the latch clicks behind him, music fades out. A shout is heard offstage.)*

BILL *(offstage):* I know I heard something down here, Mom. You'd better let me go first.

(BILL *and* JOEY *burst into the room, followed by* MRS. PAULSON, *who turns on the living-room lights. They stop in wonder when they see all the presents under the tree.* JOEY *is excited. He runs to the window, craning his neck toward the rooftop.* MRS. PAULSON *and* BILL *are equally overcome with surprise.)*

MRS. PAULSON: What on earth! Where . . . ? Who was here?

JOEY *(prancing with delight):* Look at it! Look at it! It is true! He did come. Mom, he did come. See, Billy, I told you he'd come. Wow, this is great! (BILL *looks with amazement at the new sled peeking out from under the tree branches. Then he catches sight of the manger scene. He goes over and admires it. He picks up the figure of Baby Jesus and turns it over thoughtfully.)*

BILL *(thoughtfully):* I guess Chris was right. The story, I mean . . . they didn't just make it up. I guess He did come for real. *(He puts the Christ child back in the box.)*

(MRS. PAULSON *puts her arm around* JOEY, *and the three sit together around the Christmas tree. Chimes can be heard in the distance, "Joy to the world, the Lord has come . . . ")*